News from the Kingdom of God

Meditations on *The Gospel of Thomas*

DAVID BREEDEN

WIPF & STOCK · Eugene, Oregon

NEWS FROM THE KINGDOM OF GOD
Medtiations on *The Gospel of Thomas*

Wipf & Stock
An Imprint of Wipf and Stock Publishers
199 W. 8th Ave., Suite 3
Eugene, OR 97401
www.wipfandstock.com

ISBN 13: 978-1-61097-779-1

Manufactured in the U.S.A.

Part of the introduction first appeared as "A Theology of Creativity: Theo/a/poetics" in Religious Humanism, Vol. xli n. 2, Spring 2011.

The translation included in the present book was constructed by the use of the original Coptic, consulting Michael Grondin's Coptic/English interlinear translation, revised November 22, 2002, Copyright 1997, 2002 by Michael W. Grondin. All rights reserved. http://gospel thomas.net/xtransl.htm.

New Revised Standard Version Bible, copyright 1989, Division of Christian Education of the National Council of the Churches of Christ in the United States of America. Used by permission. All rights reserved.

Unless otherwise noted, all translations are by the author.

For my children, as much as I can speak.

*It is not God that is worshipped but the authority
that claims to speak in his name. Sin becomes disobedience
to authority not violation of integrity.*

—Sarvepalli Radhakrishnan

Contents

Foreword

W HEN DAVID BREEDEN INVITED me to write a foreword to his meditations on the Gospel of Thomas, I was tempted to write, simply, *read.*

If you lean toward first thought, best thought, feel free to skip the next few paragraphs for the time being and jump in now. They'll still be here if, when you get to the end, you choose to return to this beginning.

David's translation and meditations speak for themselves, and they speak in a lively, direct tone appropriate to a peasant poet deeply attentive to the world that embraced him right where he was, painfully aware of its problems, convinced of its possibilities, passionate about its promise. David takes up this most gnostic gospel in part because the Church didn't. Since its rediscovery, the text has been an important source for interpreters hoping to find in it words of Jesus uncontained by ecclesial structures and institutions that evolved over centuries to contain them as well as proclaim them. Here, they come free of the life meticulously woven in the process of weaving a Church. Here, readers encounter a poet in his poems—or, more properly, two poets engaged in the dance translation dances at its best. The Jesus of Thomas is here, but so is the translator, a poet in this case who thinks enough of another's poems to dance them again, to invite readers to dance them again and again.

Ernesto Cardenal, another contemporary poet who has spent a great deal of time dancing about the architecture of the words at the heart of the good news Jesus was said to proclaim, has translated the words at the beginning of that good news simply and directly: *revolution now.* What follows then (and David picks this up in his citation of the Epistle of James) is being about what revolution is about, always a matter of debate. As Mark reported them, as I understand them, the words were, *God's reign is now, so close you can touch it; now turn and act as though you believed it.*

Yes, a kind of dance: *to turn, turn, will be our delight, till by turning, turning we come round right.*

Practice makes perfect, they say, and that folk wisdom is a good thought with which to begin. Jesus, particularly the Jesus of David Breeden's *Gospel of Thomas*, is a poet who, like countless rabbis and prophets before and after, believes himself part of a community that is deeded, not creeded: there is no creed but deed. By their fruits you will know them, this poet is reputed to have said in speaking of prophets true and false, and there is a bountiful harvest here.

Knowing it well, I think, will drive us out of our minds (a surprising outcome for a gnostic gospel, but this is good news that thrives on paradox), where, embodied, we can be about being the beloved community, a body that does justice, loves kindness, walks humbly, and knows nothing more divine.

Steven Schroeder
Chicago, Illinois

Acknowledgments

THANKS TO STEVEN SCHROEDER for his foreword to this book and for his suggestions on rough drafts. Thanks to the Twitter community, where many of these sayings first and cryptically appeared. Responses from interested strangers can be illuminating. Also thanks to my congregation, who has been not only kind enough to pay me as I wrote this book but also patiently listened in sermons and classes to my ruminations as these sayings percolated in my mind. Lastly, thanks to my wife, always patient with my projects.

Introduction

A New Way of Seeing

IN A LETTER DATED Sunday, 21 December 1817 to "my dear brothers," the British poet John Keats outlined his concept of how to be a great poet, which he called "Negative Capability." By this he meant a poet "capable of being in uncertainties, mysteries, doubts, without any irritable reaching after fact and reason." For Keats the great example was Shakespeare. In a great poet, "the sense of Beauty overcomes every other consideration, *or rather obliterates all consideration.*"

For me, this idea encompasses both the writing of poetry and the way of living a consciously spiritual life.

> *Uncertainties. Mysteries. Doubts.*
> *Irritable reaching. Fact. Reason.*

Both Keats and the Buddha thought these diminish our spirits. Jesus thought so too, at least the Jesus portrayed in the *Gospel of Thomas*, who is a poet, a poet teaching what Keats came to call Negative Capability.

After all, despite all efforts to cage them, the words of Jesus have never been caught. Not in the Second Century when many of the Christian scriptures were written; not in the Twelfth Century, highwater mark of Roman Catholic Europe; not at the height of Western Imperialism in the Twentieth Century; not now. All claims to a "church universal" have proven to be so much provincial bragging. The words of Jesus have never been caged.

Bookstore shelves have filled with titles containing the word "new" in front of the word "Christianity." Clearly, I am not the only "tradition Christian" who has felt a lack in Christianity. Sometime in its two thousand year journey, Christianity became more interested in the story of Jesus rising from the dead—the otherworldly magic—than the hard work of living in this world. Christianity became a set of propositions to believe in—no matter how difficult that belief became—rather than a way to live a life of peace, care, and relationship. Yet, when we turn to the words of the Gospels, the red letters of the words of Jesus, isn't it peace, care, and relationship—to the sacred and to each other—that we read about? Somehow, Christianity lost its way.

Yet, a framework survives: *metanoia, kenosis,* and *perichoresis*— changing the mind; emptying the self; joining in the dance of the sacred. That is the process Keats imagined; it is the process *The Gospel of Thomas* invites us to. There is no belief; only practice.

The Text

Scholars had long known of *The Gospel of Thomas*, though a relatively complete copy of it was not discovered until 1945. Unlike the canonized Gospels of Matthew, Mark, Luke, and John, *The Gospel of Thomas* contains no *bios*, biography. It consists, rather, of sayings or teachings of Jesus, some familiar from the Gospels, some with additions or deletions from the Gospel versions, some unknown before. Readers familiar with the canonical Gospels will be immediately struck by the similarities of many of these sayings and parables with those in other Gospels. This can be explained by one of three theories: that they are older than—and perhaps a source for—the sayings and parables that appear in the other Gospels; that they occurred in a parallel tradition that interacted little with the canonical material; or that they are derived from the Gospels for another (perhaps gnostic) purpose. What we know for sure is that the early Christian movement contained disparate and geographically dispersed traditions concerning the meaning of the life, the death, and the teachings of Jesus.

As in the case of the canonical Gospels, *The Gospel of Thomas* claims authorship by a noted historical personality, in this case Didymos Judas Thomas, one of the twelve followers, perhaps most famous as "Doubting Thomas." *Didymos* is Greek, meaning "twin." "Thomas" means "twin" in Aramaic. By tradition, Thomas was a brother of Jesus, though not necessarily the twin of Jesus. Also by tradition Thomas was the only one of the Twelve to leave the Roman Empire during his ministry, traveling to Syria, Persia, and ultimately India.

The Gospel of Thomas appears to have been originally written in Greek and later translated into Coptic. The Coptic text is the basis for this translation. It should be noted that the order of the sayings does not appear to reflect any progression of ideas toward a conclusion.

As mentioned previously, much debate circles around the composition date of *The Gospel of Thomas*. The text could be very early, perhaps even one of the sources for the *Gospel According to Mark*, earliest of the canonical Gospels. Or it could be later, about the turn of the second century, perhaps contemporaneous with the *Gospel According to John*, last written of the canonical Gospels. The date of composition makes a great deal of difference in how to understand the text. Based on a later dating of the text, *The Gospel of Thomas* has been labeled "gnostic," part of a mystical branch of Christianity later considered heretical. If it is earlier, however, predating the gnostic movement, it may contain the record of a non-Platonic mystical tradition dating to the teachings of Jesus himself. This is the assumption I have worked from in the following translation.

The controversy over the dating of the text may never be resolved. There is no doubt, however, that *The Gospel of Thomas* is fascinating as a study in mystical, non-dual thinking, a "wisdom way" that did not enter the Western consciousness again until the discovery of Eastern thought many centuries later.

A Note on the Structure of this Book

THIS TRANSLATION OF THE *Gospel of Thomas* is rendered as free verse. *The Gospel of Thomas* is made up of parables and aphorisms designed not to be prescriptive but evocative—to call out our own hearts and minds into the lived experience of the present moment. Each of the numbered sayings is designed to lead the disciples of Jesus—which now includes you—to an understanding of what has in Christian tradition been called "the kingdom of God" or "eternal life." (The phrase in Greek is *Balileia ton Ouranon*.) In the Jewish tradition of which Jesus was a part the preferred term nowadays is "the Sovereignty of Heaven." The Rev. Dr. Martin Luther King called it the Beloved Community. In this translation I have called it The Dance of the Sacred. Why call it that? Because in my lived experience, my deepest religious experiences—call them mystic, perhaps—have manifested as an invitation to join the dance of all that is. You are invited.

Meditations on *The Gospel of Thomas*

Prologue

These are the secret sayings of the living Jesus
that Didymos Judas Thomas wrote down.

Meditation

Why is it Jesus
Will speak this way?
Aphorisms and parables:

Who do they keep out?

Not the poor;
not the uneducated;
not those in pain.

Rather, those left out
are those unwilling
to consider paradox;
those who already
"know it all."

1

He said:

Whoever realizes the meaning of these words,
that person will never die.

Meditation

The Buddhist poet Nagarjuna said something similar,

Nothing comes into existence
and nothing disappears.
Nothing is eternal;
nothing ever ends.
Nothing is identical
and nothing is different.

Nothing moves here or there.

2

Jesus said:

Do not stop until you find.
And when you find,
you will be troubled.

Yet, having been troubled,
you will become amazed,

and then you will be
master of all.

Meditation: Bobbing on Surfaces

Because of your bother
With the surfaces,

The old masters say,
You have lost what is basic,

What is bright,
What is wonderful
About your own mind.

You have covered it,
Losing it like a coin.

And so it feels
Like you are on a wheel;

And so it feels

Like treading water
In an endless sea, bobbing.

Find, right now,
The old masters say,

Your own
Bright mind.

3

Jesus said:

If leaders say, "Look, the Dance of the Sacred is in the sky!"
Then notice how the birds get there before you.
If they say, "Look, the Dance of the Sacred is in the sea!"
Then notice how the fish get there before you.

No—the Dance of the Sacred is both within you and without you.
When you know yourself, then you will be known,
And you will see that you are a child of the one.

However, if you do not know yourself,
Then you live in poverty,
And you are the poverty.

Meditation

In the *Gospel According to Mark* the location and meaning of the "Kingdom of God" or Dance of the Sacred is not clear. Is it a state of mind? A function of enlightened consciousness? Is it what is known in Buddhism as the "one-mind point of view"? Is it a group of words designed to express the inexpressible? Perhaps. The kingdom is found through self-examination. The method of this self-examination follows the mystic path. As Gershon Winkler says of the Kabbalah,

> No wisdom comes to us when we are filled with it. Wisdom only comes when we are void of it, when we have hollowed out a clear space in our selves, and created room for experience and for what experience teaches us. (48)

In Christian mysticism this process is called *kenosis,* "emptying." Buddhist thought sums the ideas up in two terms in an "eightfold path" toward enlightenment: *right* (or "proper") *understanding and right mindfulness.*

4

Jesus said:

An old one will not hesitate to ask a baby
seven days old about the source of life.
And that person shall thrive.

There are many who are first
who shall be last,

and the two shall be
one and the same.

Meditation

Old/young is one duality. First/last another. One/two another. To realize
the Dance, all must become one: the one or the all.
In the first chapter of Ecclesiastes we read these words:

> What is the product of all our labors under the sun? One
> generation passes away and another generation rises; but
> the earth abides on and on. The sun also rises and the sun
> goes down, hastening again to the place where it arose. The
> wind blows toward the south, then turns to the north; it
> whirls about continually, and the wind returns again and
> again according to its circuits.
>
> All the rivers run into the sea, yet the sea is not full; unto
> the place from whence the rivers came, there they return.
> Everything is full of trouble; the tongue cannot express
> how much trouble. The eye is not satisfied in its seeing; the
> ear is not filled with hearing.

That which has been, that is what shall be; and that which has been done is that which shall be done: there is no new thing under the sun.

Is there anything of which it can be said, "Look, that is new?" No—it has been seen before. There is no remembrance of things past, nor shall there be remembrance of things to come.

5

Jesus said:

See what is in front of your face;
Then, what is hidden will be revealed.

Nothing hidden will fail to appear.

Meditation

Jesus insists that the Dance is hidden in plain sight, only requiring a closer, clearer look to recognize or dis-cover.

Chapter 11 of Hebrews begins,

> Faith is the substance of things hoped for,
> The evidence for things unseen.
> Our forebears received approval in faith.
> Through faith we understand
> That the worlds were built
> By the word of God
> In such a way that
> What we see is not what
> The worlds are made of.

As poet Emily Dickinson put it,

> Faith is a fine invention
> When Gentlemen can see—
> But Microscopes are prudent
> In an Emergency. (#185)

6

His followers asked Jesus:

Do you want us to fast?
How should we go about praying?
Should we give to charity?
Should we abstain from certain foods?

Jesus answered:
Do not tell lies.
Do not do what you hate.

Under heaven, everything is revealed—
Nothing hidden will fail to appear.

No, nothing covered will fail to be revealed.

Meditation

As we know from the canonical Gospels, religious authorities questioned the disciples of Jesus concerning their failure to observe basic purity laws. In answer to fairly concrete questions, Jesus offers more examples of the thinking in the first five sayings—all is one. What does this have to do with fasting, praying, charity, and diet?

The radical shift that Jesus purposes—from orthopraxis (right-doing) to orthodoxy (right-thinking) has become such a basic feature of Western individualism that we can miss how radical this reorientation was.

For more on the same subject, see saying #14.

7

Jesus said:

Fortunate is the lion that a human eats,
because that lion becomes human.

Cursed is the human that a lion eats,
because that human becomes a lion.

Meditation

Sufi tradition contains this story:

> Once a tiger was pursuing a man. The man ran and ran
> but could not escape the tiger. Finally, in desperation, the
> man stopped, turned, and screamed to the tiger, "Why
> don't you stop chasing me?"
>
> The tiger replied, "Why don't you stop being so appetizing?"

8

Jesus said:

A wise fisherman cast his net into the sea.
He pulled it up full of little fish.
Yet among the small, the wise fisherman
found a good, large fish.

He threw the small fish back,
Keeping the large one.

Those with ears, let them hear.

Meditation

What is the net?
Is it the words
We weave to catch
The truth with?

And there
Among the small
We find larger . . .
What?

Meaning?
Or something else?

9

Jesus said:

Listen—a man came out to sow seeds.
He took handfuls and cast the seeds.
Some seeds fell upon the road;
the birds came and ate those.

Other seeds fell onto rocks,
and those did not send roots into the earth
nor did they send shafts rising into the sky.

And some seeds fell into thorns,
which choked the seeds,
and the worms ate them.

And other seeds fell upon good earth,
and those gave fruit up to the sky.

And the sower got sixty times yield from some
and one hundred-twenty times yield from others.

Meditation

The Gospels of Matthew, Mark, and Luke all contain this parable, with the Jesus of Mark later explaining the parable to his disciples: "The sower sows the word." This is the understanding that has come down to us through Christian tradition.

What if, however, the sower sows fire, as in the following saying . . .

10

Jesus said:

I have cast fire
upon the world;
look, I watch
as it burns.

Meditation

What if fire
Is the seeds
The sower casts?

What if fire
Is the word?
What if

What's sown
Is thinking anew?

In 1 Samuel 10, Samuel tells the young Saul this,

> . . . as you come to the town, you will meet a band of proph-
> ets coming down from the shrine with harp, tambourine,
> flute, and lyre playing in front of them; they will be in a
> prophetic frenzy. Then the spirit of the Lord will possess
> you, and you will be in a prophetic frenzy along with them
> and be turned into a different person.

11

Jesus said:

This sky will pass away,
and the sky above that
will pass away.

Those who are dead do not live,
and those who live will not die.

When you eat what is dead,
you make it alive.
When you come to be in light,
what will you do?

When you were one,
you became two;
but when you become two,
what will you do?

Meditation

Meister Eckert said,

> We fight the dark
> Not knowing that
> The knower
> And the known
> Are one. Confused

People imagine—
Meister Eckert, mystic,
Said this somewhere—that
Confused people see
The sacred as if it stood
Over there and we here.

And so it is
We fight the dark,
Thinking and thinking
That the sacred is there,

Not here.
Meister Eckert said,
The sacred and I—
(Which means the sacred
And you
And me)

We are—the sacred and us—we are

One in knowledge.

12

His followers said to Jesus:

We know that you will leave us.
Who will lead us then?

Jesus answered:

Wherever you are,
turn to James the Just,
for whose sake heaven
and earth came into being.

Meditation

In the Book of James we read,

> What profit is it, my sisters and brothers, when we say we
> have faith but we have no works? Can faith save us?

> If a sister or brother is naked and destitute of daily food,
> and if one of you says to that person, "Depart in peace, be
> you warmed and filled," yet you do not give that person
> those things that a body needs, what profit is your faith?

> Even so faith, if it has not works, is dead by itself. Yes,
> someone might say, "You have faith, and I have works:
> show me your faith without your works, and I will show
> you my faith by my works."

> You believe that there is one God; in that, you do well; but the
> demons also believe this, and tremble. But will you under-
> stand, oh hollow person, that faith without works is dead?

Was not our father Abraham justified by works when he had offered his son Isaac upon the altar? See how faith created his works and by works his faith was made complete?

This is how the scripture was fulfilled that says, "Abraham believed God, and it was reckoned unto him as righteousness."

Abraham was called the friend of God. So, you see how works justify a person, not faith alone.

Likewise, was not Rahab the prostitute justified by works when she had received the messengers and had sent them out another way?

For as the body without the spirit is dead, so faith without works is dead also.

13

Jesus said:

Think of metaphors.
　　What am I like?

Simon Peter said:
　　You are like an angelic messenger.

Matthew said:
　　You are like a philosopher.

Thomas said:
　　Teacher, my tongue cannot tell what you are like.

Jesus said:
　　Thomas, I am not your teacher.
　　You are intoxicated on the bubbling spring
　　that I have measured out.

Then Jesus took Thomas aside and said three things to him.

When Thomas returned to the group,
　　they asked him what Jesus had told him.

Thomas said:
　　If I spoke to you even one of the things he spoke,
　　you would take stones and throw them at me
　　and a fire would come out of the stones and incinerate you.

Meditation

After Zen Master Hsu Yun

   Here's truth for you—
Saints are like everybody else.
Everybody else.

Finding a difference is like
Buying a ticket
When you wrote the play.

Every truth thrives
In a human heart.
It rains, the flowers perk up.

After you see what the lies are
You will paint with all
The colors of life and death.

14

Jesus said to them:

If you fast, you will bring sin upon yourselves;
and if you pray, you will be condemned by others,
and if you should give to charity, you will do damage to your spirits.

When you go out into the world,
when people invite you in,
eat what is put in front of you
and heal the sick among those people.

For what goes in your mouth does not defile you;
rather it is what comes out of your mouth that might defile you.

Meditation

Whenever these persistent questions arise, Jesus turns the questions around. In this Jesus joins with other Hebrew prophets, such as Amos, speaking in God's voice:

> I hate, I despise your festivals, and I take no delight in your solemn assemblies. Even though you offer me your burnt offerings and grain offerings, I will not accept them; and the offerings of well-being of your fatted animals I will not look upon. Take away from me the noise of your songs; I will not listen to the melody of your harps. But let justice roll down like waters, and righteousness like an ever-flowing stream. (Amos 5:21-24: NRSV)

As the Buddha put it in *The Dhammapada*, considered to be a record of the spoken words of the Buddha,

We ourselves make the bad; we ourselves make the impure.

We ourselves unmake the bad; we ourselves unmake the
  impure.
We ourselves make the pure and the impure.
No one can do this for another.

15

Jesus said:

When you see someone not born of woman,
fall down and worship that one.
That one is The One.

Meditation

Meister Eckert referred to this unmediated, non-material condition as "a
light in the soul that is uncreated."

16

Jesus said:

Perhaps people think
I have come to sow peace
over the world.

They do not understand
I have come to cast division
upon the earth—

fire, sword, and war.

There will be five in a house.
There will be three opposing two
and two against three. Father
will oppose son and son oppose father.

Each will stand
and each will stand
alone.

Meditation

This saying appears (in altered form) in both Matthew 10:34-36 and
Luke 12:51–53. It does not occur in Mark and is therefore part of what
scholars have come to call the Q Source, a conjectural source for the
common elements in Matthew and Luke that do not appear in Mark. *The
Gospel of Thomas* may be a version of the Q Source. Be that as it may, in
all three appearances of these words, the warning is clear: following the
way of Jesus has consequences.

17

Jesus said:

I will give you what
eyes have not seen,
ears have not heard,
hands have not touched,
minds have not thought.

Meditation

The Void. The Tao. The One. What is "the truth"? The *Babylonian Talmud* describes a question put to Rabbi Akiva: "Is all preordained or do human beings have free will?"

The rabbi replied, "It is all preordained, and the choice is yours."

18

His followers said:

Tell us about the end.
How will it happen?

Jesus said:

Have you found the beginning?
Is that why you look for the end?
Where the beginning is,
there is the end.

Fortunate are those who stand on two feet at the beginning
and will therefore know the end, never tasting death.

Meditation

Unlike the Jesus of the Gospels, who shows millennialist tendencies and
readily speculates on an "end time," the Jesus of *The Gospel of Thomas*
teaches that all time is eternity. Both personal death and "The End of the
World" disappear in the eternal present that is life in the all.

As E.E. Cummings said of divinity in his poem "i am a little church (no
great cathedral),"

> merciful Him Whose only now is forever

19

Jesus said:

Fortunate are those who came into being before coming into being.
If you become my follower and listen to my words, these stones will
    serve you.

There are five trees in paradise
that do not change from summer to winter
and do not lose their leaves.
Those who know them will not taste death.

Meditation

Words prove to be very problematic vehicles for carrying our ideas, re-
vealing our emotions, or expressing religious insight. Still, we continue
to try. Mystics have long held that their experiences lie in a realm beyond words.

What does the phrase "five trees of paradise" mean? Is it the five senses?
Is it a delineation of mental conditions toward mystic insight? (Perhaps
sanity plus reason plus mindfulness plus imagination plus intention—
equals experiencing the real.) We do not know. Yet it appears to have
been an important concept in the teachings of Jesus, at least the teachings recorded in *The Gospel of Thomas*.

20

His followers said to Jesus:

What is the Dance of the Sacred like?

Jesus said to them:

It is like a mustard seed,
smallest of seeds. However,
when a mustard seed falls on good earth
it sends out branches
and becomes a shelter
for the birds of the sky.

Meditation

The most famous simile for the Dance of the Sacred: Small. Weed-like.
Gets no respect. Yet, it functions as a tree.

21

Mary asked Jesus:

What are your followers like?

Jesus said:
    They are like small children living in a field that is not theirs.
    When the owners of the field come, they will say, "Give us our field
        back!"
    The children will strip naked right in front of the owners
    and give the field back to them.

Therefore, I tell you this:
    If the owner of a house knows a thief is coming,
    the owner will keep an eye open so that the thief does not sneak in
        and steal things.

You must always keep watch on the world.
Arm yourselves with strength so that thieves will not ambush you,
though the defense you have will be the defense that is attacked.
Keep those with understanding in your midst always.

When the grain was ripe, the farmer hurried out
with his sickle in his hand,
in order to reap.
Those with ears, let them hear.

Meditation

In Luke 6:29 Jesus puts it this way,

    To the one who strikes you on one cheek, offer the other;
    From the one who takes your cloak, do not save back your
        coat.

22

Jesus saw some babies nursing.

He said to his followers:
    These little ones having milk,
    they are like those who enter into the Dance.

His followers said to Jesus:
    Then we will enter into the Dance if we are babies?

Jesus said to them:
    When you make two one,
    and when you make inside like outside,
    and outside like inside,
    and top like bottom,
    and male like female,
    so that there is no male or female;
    when you make eyes that replace eyes,
    hands that replace hands,
    feet that replace feet,
    images that replace images,

    then you will join the Dance.

Meditation

Saying #22 is key to grasping the mode of thinking in *The Gospel of Thomas*. Male/female is another binary that has no place in the Dance of the Sacred. (See the final saying, #114.)

As Dogen, founder of the Soto school of Zen Buddhism, put it, "When one no longer divides mind and object, the gate of liberation is open." Zen master Dazu Huike carried it a step further:

> The unenlightened
> and the enlightened
> are one and the same,
> not separate at all.
> We must realize that
> all things are as they are.

23

Jesus said:

I will choose you,
One out of a thousand,
Two out of ten thousand.

You will stand on your feet
As if you were one.

Meditation

Few get it, be they Jewish, Christian, Muslim, Hindu, Buddhist, *et cetera*.
Atheists get there too. As atheist philosopher Andre Comte-Sponville
puts it,

> That everything contained by the all is relative and condi-
> tioned, as I believe to be the case, does not imply that the
> all itself is relative and conditioned; indeed, if it is truly the
> all, that possibility is excluded. (139)

Chinese Taoist philosopher Zhuangzi wrote,

> There is no self
> And no other-than-self.
> There is nothing
> Hard about The Way—
> Just stop making distinctions!
>
> After you do not love or hate,
> The Way will appear, clear to you.
> Stop being for or against;
> Stop hoping; stop hating.
> These are diseases of the mind.

When we do not know
The meaning of things,
We disturb our original minds
For no reason at all.

24

His followers said to Jesus:

Show us the place where you are, since we must get there too.

Jesus said to them:
    Those with ears, let them hear.
    There is light inside a person of light
    that becomes light to the world.

Those who shine no light are darkness.

Meditation

Alfred North Whitehead said,

    It is the function of actuality
    to characterize the creativity,
    and God is the eternal primordial character.
    But, of course, there is no meaning
    to "creativity" apart from its "creatures,"
    and no meaning to "god"
    apart from the "creativity"
    and the "temporal creatures,"
    and no meaning to the "temporal creatures"
    apart from "creativity" and "God."
    (line breaks added)

The book of Genesis puts it a bit more eloquently:

    In the beginning Elohim created heaven and earth.
    The earth was void and empty
    and darkness was upon the deep
    and the spirit of Elohim moved upon the water.

Then Elohim said,
"Let there be light,"
and there was light.

And Elohim saw the light,
that it was good,
& divided the light from the darkness
and called the light day
and the darkness night,

and so of the evening and morning was made the first day
. . .

25

Jesus said:

Love your companions like your soul.
Guard them as if they were the pupil of your eye.

Meditation

In Buddhism the Three Jewels or Three Treasures, the gifts of Buddhism, are the Buddha, the Dharma, and the Sangha. That is, the sayings and example of the Buddha, the Way or practice of Buddhism, and a group of fellow practitioners. *The Gospel of Thomas* shows Three Treasures for the followers of Jesus: The sayings and example of Jesus; the practice of the Dance of the Sacred, and the cohesion of a group of followers. (See saying #12.)

In her last novel, *The Waves*, Virginia Woolf has a character say, "some people go to priests; others to poetry; I to my friends." This elegantly simple sentence insightfully sums up the ways we human beings may search for "truth." We can go to the great religious traditions; we can go to the vast archive of accumulated human creativity; we can go to our friends. In *The Gospel of Thomas* Jesus and his disciples do all three.

26

Jesus said:

You see the speck in your companion's eye,
but you do not see the beam in your own.

If you first get the beam out of your eye,
then you will see well enough to
get the speck out of your companion's eye.

Meditation

This saying, which also appears in the canonical Gospels, gets my vote for the best articulation of a central human fault—criticism or judgment of others. Zen master Dogen said, "Do not speak of the errors and faults of others. Do not destroy The Way."

27

Jesus said:

If you do not fast from the world,
you will not find the Dance;

if you do not treat the Sabbath
as Sabbath, you will not see the One.

Meditation

The Sufi poet Rumi told the story of a scholar named Wasim who once chanced to hear a shepherd praying. The shepherd's prayer went something like this: "God, I wish I knew where you are, because I would like to polish your shoes and comb your hair for you."

"Who do you think you are talking to?" the wise Wasim asked.

"To God," the shepherd said.

"Well," said Wasim, "that is no way to talk to God. God doesn't have shoes or hair, and it is silly to pray in that manner."

The shepherd, embarrassed to have been overheard by such a wise and learned man, slunk off the road and into the desert.

Wasim continued walking down the road until he heard the voice of God, saying, "Wasim, what do you think you are doing? You just separated one of my children from me. What is wrong for one is good for another. What people *do* in worship means nothing to me. Worship is for the worshiper, not for me. Some people are philosophers, some are lovers. It makes no difference to me."

Wasim immediately ran after the shepherd, following his footprints through the sand. When finally he found the shepherd, Wasim said, "I am so sorry. I was wrong in what I said. Your prayers are special to God."

The shepherd stopped walking and said, "No. Thank you for scolding me. Now I see. When we look into a mirror, we see ourselves, not the condition of the mirror. It is the flute player, not the flute that makes music."

Wasim suddenly realized that when finally we see through this veil we call reality, we will certainly say, "Huh! That's not the way I thought it was."

28

Jesus said:

I have taken my stand in the world;
I have appeared in the flesh.
And I found everyone drunk;
no one is thirsty. My soul

was pained for the children of the earth,
for they are blind in their hearts.
They do not look outside themselves.
They came into the world empty,
and they seek to leave the world empty.

For now, they are drunk;
when they sober up,
they will see.

Meditation

The anonymous author of the great medieval mediation manual *The Cloud of Unknowing* put it this way:

> All those who set out to be spiritual workers within (their
> own souls) and suppose they can hear, smell, see, taste, or
> feel spiritual things—either within the body or without
> it—surely are deceived and work against the course of na-
> ture. For nature has ordained that through nature we will
> know all outward, bodily things, but in no wise by those
> will we arrive at knowing spiritual things.

I mean by their works. By their failings we may know spiritual things, for this reason: when we tell others or hear from others of some certain things, we sometimes realize that our outward wits cannot tell us by any sense-quality what those things are. When this happens, we may be very certain that those things are spiritual things, not bodily things.

In this same manner, in spiritual things we go to our spiritual wits when we try hard to know God Himself. For no matter how much spiritual understanding we have, still we can never by the work of our understandings arrive at the knowing of an un-made spiritual thing, which is nothing but God.

But by failing we may know, because the thing that we fail at is nothing else but only God. This is why Saint Denis said: "The best knowing of God is that which is known by unknowing."

29

Jesus said:

If flesh comes into being
because of spirit,
that is a wonder;

if spirit comes into being
because of the body,
that is a wondrous wonder.

What amazes me
is that this great richness
thrives in this poverty.

Meditation

Jesus draws a distinction between the created world—the material reality—and the uncreated, unmediated eternal reality. The soul—the unmediated—does not "manifest" body; neither does the material "manifest" the eternal. In other sayings, however, Jesus does not take a dim view of material reality as such, only our propensity to assume that it is all or enough.

Chapter 40 of the *Tao Teh Ching* (Dao De Jing) says,

> The events of the world arise from the determinate
> And the determinate arises from the indeterminate.
> (Ames 139)

30

Jesus said:

Wherever there are
three gods,
they are gods;
wherever there are
two or one,

I am with them.

Meditation

The "one-mind point of view" is necessarily "monotheistic" in a fundamental sense. As Sufi poet Hafiz puts it, "all our tambourines strike one
knee."

31

Jesus said:

No prophet is accepted in his own village;
no physician heals those who know the physician.

Meditation

In the Gospels we have a context for this saying—Jesus revisiting his hometown of Nazareth and finding suspicion and rejection there. See saying #86.

Luke 9:58-62 reads,

> Jesus said to another, "Follow me."
> The man said, "Master, allow me first to go and bury
>   my father."
> Jesus said to him, "Let the dead bury their dead—go and
> preach the kingdom of God."
> Another said, "Lord, I will follow you, but first allow me to
> say farewell to those at my house."
> Jesus said to him, "No one who has put his hand to the
> plow and then looks back is fit for the kingdom of God."

32

Jesus said:

A city built and fortified on a mountain cannot be hidden.

Meditation

Matthew 5:14-16 reads,

> You are the light of the world. A city set on a hill cannot be hid. Neither does someone light a candle and put it under a basket, but on a candlestick so that it gives light to everyone in the house. Let your light so shine before humanity, so that they may see your good works and glorify your God, who is in heaven.

(See the following saying.)

33

Jesus said:

What you hear,
preach that
from the housetops;

for is there anyone
who lights a lamp and
puts it under a basket?

No, we put it on a lampstand
so everyone can see the light.

Meditation

We must tell our truth. The teacher of Ecclesiastes said,

> In my heart I said, "Come—I will try mirth—enjoy your-
> self!" Behold—this also is empty air.

> I said of laughter, "It is mad!" and of mirth, "What is the
> point?" I tried to dedicate myself to wine, yet still I thirsted
> for wisdom rather than folly, wondering what is best for
> humanity to do under heaven all the days of life.

> I created great things: I built houses; I planted vineyards:
> I made gardens and orchards and planted trees in them of
> all kinds. I made pools of water for nurturing the trees; I
> hired servants and maids, and there were servants born in
> my house; also I had many animals, great and small, more
> than anyone in Jerusalem before me. I gathered silver and
> gold, and the peculiar treasure of kings from the provinces;
> I hired singers, both women and men, and musical instru-
> ments, and all the earthly delights.

Thus I was great, greater than anyone before me in Jerusalem. Furthermore, I remained wise. Whatsoever my eyes desired, I got it. I withheld not my heart from any joy; for my heart rejoiced in all my works and in the product of all my works.

Then I looked on all the works that my hands had wrought, and on the things that I had worked to do, and, behold, all was empty air and vexation of spirit. I saw that there is nothing to be gained under the sun.

So I turned myself to the study of wisdom, madness, and folly: for what can anyone do that a king cannot?

Then I realized that anyone can only do what has already been done.

Wisdom surpasses folly, as far as light surpasses darkness. The wise one's eyes are in his head; but the fool walks in darkness. I perceived that one event happens to them all. Then I said in my heart, "As it happens to the fool, so it happens even to me; and so how is it that I am more wise?" (Chapter 2)

34

Jesus said:

When the blind lead the blind, they all fall into a pit.

Meditation

One-eyed rulers have not done much better. As the *Tao Teh Ching* says,

> To win the world, one must renounce all.
> If one still has private ends to serve,
> One will never be able to win the world.
> (John C.H. Wu 71)

35

Jesus said:

It is impossible to go into a strong man's house
and steal his goods unless he is bound first.

Then his things can be stolen.

Meditation

Jewish tradition contains the story of two sheep swimming across a
river. One had been shorn; the other had its full fleece. The sheep with
its fleece grew heavy and drowned; the shorn sheep survived.

36

Jesus said:

Do not worry from morning until evening
and evening until morning about what you will wear.

Meditation

Matthew 6:28 continues,

> Consider the lilies of the field, how they grow;
> they toil not, neither do they spin . . .

Here we do not see this organic comparison, since the Jesus of *The Gospel of Thomas* is not recommending a simple life per se. Rather, our challenge is to find a way past or outside of all material concerns. To worry is to miss the sustenance of the Dance of the Sacred. Is such a frame of mind possible? As Zen Master John Daido Loori put it,

> All of our machinations, grabbing, controlling, and dominating; all of our squabbling and struggling to get, to hoard, to take, is an upside-down way of understanding the nature of the universe and the nature of the self. Be giving. (68)

37

His followers said:

When will you appear to us?
Which day will we see you?

Jesus said:
    When you strip yourselves naked without being ashamed,
      and you take your garments and stand on them like little children,
        trampling them, then you will look upon the Child of The One
          Who Lives

and you will not be afraid.

Meditation

Saying #21 also predicts nakedness and a lack of shame. To the question of "when," Jesus describes the state of mind required of the coming of the Dance of the Sacred. In saying #21, the coming implies a lack of fear in the face of the oppressors. Here, all shame has gone.

Chiao Jan, Monk, said,

    How is it
    We talk the end

    Before we hit the shore?

    It is the rowing—

    Autumn wind
    Hard

    On the water.

38

Jesus said:

You have many times desired
to hear these words
I am saying to you,

and you have no one else to say them to you.

There will be days
you seek for me
and will not find me.

Meditation

In *The Dhammapada* the Buddha says,

> People love their obstacles.
> Only the enlightened get past them.

39

Jesus said:

The religious authorities and the scholars
have taken the keys to knowledge and hidden them.

They have not entered,
nor do they allow those
who desire knowledge to enter.

You, however, will be
cunning like snakes and
innocent like doves.

Meditation

See saying # 102.

Spiritual philosopher Jiddu Krishnamurti said,

> In oneself lies the whole world and if you know how to
> look and learn, the door is there and the key is in your
> hand. Nobody on earth can give you either the key or the
> door to open, except yourself.

40

Jesus said:

They have planted a grapevine outside of The One,
    but it will have no nourishment

and it will be uprooted and destroyed.

Meditation

This saying, along with sayings #9 and #57, all describe the consequences of good seeds meeting with bad seeds or bad soil. The Buddha said,

> Just as a vine may strangle a tree,
> Just so may our actions choke us . . .

41

Jesus said:

Whoever has will get more;
whoever does not have, even

that little will be taken.

Meditation

As Zen Master John Daido Loori puts it,

> If you have a staff I will give you one.
> If you don't have a staff, I'll take it away. (55)

42

Jesus said:

Be by passing by.

Meditation

The gist of this elegantly simple phrase is tough to get. In a longer articulation, it would be something like, "Come into being as you pass through (this life)." There is, however, a poetry to the phrasing that is difficult to catch.

The teaching is to balance the transience of life with the eternal moment of the now. The fullest realization or articulation of spirit lies in acceptance, "going with the flow."

43

His followers said to Jesus:

Who are you, that you say these things to us?

Jesus said:

When I speak these things,
you do not realize who I am.
Rather, you are like those Judeans
who love the tree
yet hate the fruit or
love the fruit yet hate the tree.

Meditation

In *The Gospel of Thomas* we do not hear the "I am" statements so familiar from *The Gospel According to John*. Rather than claiming authority based on knowing the mind of God, the Jesus of *The Gospel of Thomas* focuses on thought and action. Loving Jesus as "the Christ" without heeding his words and actions is missing half the story.

The Buddha, upon being asked if he were divine, responded, "No, I am awake."

44

Jesus said:

Whoever curses against the one
Will be forgiven;

Whoever curses against the son
Will be forgiven;

Whoever curses against the holy spirit,
However, will not be forgiven,

Not on earth, not in the sky.

Meditation

The continuing fluid actions of the Spirit in the world must not be gain-said. In Chapter 38 of the book of *Job*, God speaks from a whirlwind:

> "Who is this who talks without knowing?
> Get some clothes on, like a man.
> I have some questions
> And I expect you to answer.
> Just where were you when I laid the foundations of the earth?
> Tell me, if you have any answers.
>
> "Just who planned the earth? Do you know
> Who stretched out the plumb line?
>
> "What are the foundations of the world fastened to?
> Who laid the cornerstone of the earth
> On that day when the morning stars sang together,

And all the sons of God shouted for joy?

"Who was it shut up the doors of the sea
When those broke open and the water
Rushed out, as if from a womb?

"Who was it made the clouds
Like clothing for the earth
And the darkness like swaddling clothes,
And set the outer boundaries
And set bars and doors?

"Who said to the waves,
'You can come this far and no farther?'
Have you commanded the morning in your lifetime
And made the daylight keep its place?

"Have you been to the springs of the sea?
Have you walked in the sea's depths?
Have the gates of death been opened to you?
Have you seen the doors of the shadow of death?
Have you seen the breadth of the earth?
Tell me if you know . . .

"Where does light dwell?
And as for darkness . . . where does it live?
Do you know the way to those houses?
Were you born when these things happened?
Are you that old?

"Have you ever visited the storehouse of the snow?
Have you seen the storehouse of the hail
That I keep in reserve for battles and wars?

"Which is the road to the place the light is parted
And the east wind is scattered on the earth?

"Who was it made the courses for the rain
Or a way for lightning and thunder
So that it falls upon the earth,
Even in the places no person lives
So that the tender buds of the herb can grow?

"Does the rain have a father?
Whose child is the drop of dew?
Who is the mother of the ice
And the frosts of heaven
That make water turn to stone
And freeze the face of the deep?

"Can you chain the Pleiades
Or free the shackles of Orion?
Can you bring out the constellations in their seasons?
Can you guide Arcturus with his sons?

"Do you know the laws of heaven?
Might you make the earth obey them?
Can you lift your voice to the clouds and bring down rain?
Can you send lightning bolts wherever you please?

"Who has taught the rules to all things?
Who gave wisdom to the human heart?
Who is wise enough to number the clouds?
Who can open the jars of heaven
When the dust grows hard
And the clods stick together?

"Will you do the hunting for a lion
When her cubs are hungry
And they crouch in their dens
Lying quietly in wait?

"Who feeds the raven
When his young ones
Cry to God, wandering in starvation?"

45

Jesus said:

No one harvests grapes out of thorns.
Nor does anyone gather figs out of thistles.
Those do not produce fruit.

Good people bring good things from their storehouses;
bad people bring bad and wicked things from theirs,
meaning from their hearts.

From the excesses of their hearts they bring evil things.

Meditation

Chapter 71 of the *Tao Teh Ching* says,

> Knowing that one does not know is knowing at its best,
> But not knowing that one knows is suffering from a
> disease.
> Thus, the reason the sages are free of disease
> Is because they recognize the disease as a disease.
> This is why they are not afflicted. (Ames 189)

46

Jesus said:

From Adam up to John the Baptist,
among those born of women,
no one has been more worthy of respect
than John the Baptist.

Still any of you who
becomes like a little child
will know the Dance and be
more worthy of respect than John.

Meditation

The composer John Cage said, "I can't understand why people are frightened of new ideas. I'm frightened of the old ones."

47

Jesus said:

No way can anyone climb onto two horses or stretch two bows.
No way can a servant serve two masters.

He will honor one and despise the other.

No one drinks aged wine and immediately desires new wine.
No one pours new wine into old wine skins because they would split
    open.
Nor does anyone pour old wine into new wineskins because that would
    ruin the wine.

No one sews old patches to new garments because that would tear
    them.

Meditation

Taoist Wei Wu Wei said,

> Why are you unhappy?
> Because 99.9 per cent
> Of everything you think,
> And of everything you do,
> Is for yourself—
> And there isn't one.

48

Jesus said:

Should two make peace
with each other in this house,
they will be able to speak

to a mountain saying,
"Move away,"
and the mountain will move.

Meditation

The Dance of the Universe is like two men talking over coffee, sitting by
a beautiful blooming tree. The blooms blow into their mouths, into their
coffee, yet they laugh and talk on.

See Saying #106.

49

Jesus said:

Fortunate are those
who are alone and chosen,
for they will find the Dance.

Since they are from it,
they are going back to it.

Meditation

> As with wheat
> It is not after falling
> Alone but also in falling
> We find the ground

50

Jesus said:

If they should ask you, "Where have you come from?"
Say this—"We have come from the light,
From the place where the light came into being,
Made by its own hand,
Standing forth in its image."

If they should ask you, "Are you The One?"
Say this—"We are his children, chosen by the living One."

If they should ask you, "What is the sign that the One is in you?"
Say this to them—"It is motion and stillness."

Meditation: The Morning of the World

> When you know your point
> Of view is a blind spot;
>
> When your this is your that;
> When your yes and your no
> Lope off, caressing;
>
> When your here is as well as your there;
> When your good is just as bad;
>
> When your opposites
> Aren't any more;
>
> When you know you are sitting
> On the limb you are sawing off
> Like any animated character;

When you watch yes and no romp
Off your leash without shouting;

When the flags of inevitable armies
Are the stuff of dreaming;

When all the words
Of all the prophets

Are so many warbles in the song;
When your dance is where you rest serene . . .

Open those other eyes;
Look—
It is the morning of the world.

51

His followers said to Jesus:

When will the dead rest?
When will the new world appear?

Jesus said to them:

What you have been looking for has come,
But you do not know it.

Meditation

In Luke 17:21 Jesus says, "Neither shall they say, 'Look here!' or, 'Look there!'" for, behold, the Kingdom of God is within you."

In Christian tradition this is theosis, or "divinization." 2 Peter 1:4 says,

> Whereby are given unto us exceeding great and precious promises: that by these ye might be partakers of the divine nature, having escaped the corruption that is in the world through lust. (KJV)

This "partaking" in the divine nature is the mystical way.

52

His followers said to Jesus:

Twenty four prophets have spoken in Israel, and they spoke about you.

Jesus said to them:
> Speaking only about the dead, you have left out the living one who is in your presence.

Meditation

The author of *The Cloud of Unknowing* says,

> Lift up your heart into God with a meek stirring of love and think only of Himself and none of the good He can do. Loath to look on anything but Himself, so that nothing works in your mind or in your will but only Himself. Forget all the creatures that God ever made and the works they have done, so that neither your thoughts nor your desires are directed or stretched toward any of them, neither in general nor in particular. Just let them be and take no notice of them. (Chapter 3)

53

His followers said to Jesus:

Is circumcision beneficial to us or not?

Jesus said to them:

Were it beneficial, children would be born circumcised.
Rather, circumcision of the spirit is what is beneficial.

Meditation

As we have seen, outward manifestations are the product of inner light,
not the other way around.

The author of *The Cloud of Unknowing* instructs:

> Work firmly in this nothing and this nowhere, and leave
> your outward bodily wits and all that they deal with; for I
> tell you truly that this work may not be conceived by them.
> Consider: by your eyes you may not conceive of anything
> except by such things as the length and the breadth, the
> smallness and the greatness, the roundness and the square-
> ness, the farness and the nearness, and the color. And by
> your ears you may not conceive of anything except noise
> or some type of sound. By your nose you may not conceive
> of anything except by stench or savor. By your taste, only
> by sour or sweet, salt or fresh, bitter or tasty. By your feel-
> ing you may not conceive of anything except either hot or
> cold, hard or tender, soft or sharp. Truly neither God nor
> spiritual things have any of these qualities or quantities!
> Therefore leave your outward wits—don't work with them,
> either within or without.

All those who set out to be spiritual workers within (their own souls) and suppose they can hear, smell, see, taste, or feel spiritual things—either within the body or without it—surely are deceived and work against the course of nature. For nature has ordained that through nature we will know all outward, bodily things, but in no wise by those shall we arrive at knowing spiritual things. (Chapter 70)

54

Jesus said:

Fortunate are the poor, for yours is the Dance of the Sacred.

Meditation

In Medieval England an anonymous poet wrote this,

Praise of Contentment with Little

High towers by strong winds are dashed
While low cottages stand sure & fast
Therefore be sure it's better in poverty to hide
Than hastily to be rich and suddenly to slide.

55

Jesus said:

Whoever does not hate
both father and mother
cannot become my follower.

Whoever does not hate
both brothers and sisters—
whoever does not take up
a cross as I do—
is not deserving of me.

Meditation

The most famous conversion story, the story of how Saul the persecutor became Paul the apostle, occurs in the book of *Acts*, Chapter 9:

> Saul, spewing threats and slaughter against the disciples of the Lord, went to the high priest asking for letters to the Damascus synagogues so that if he found any followers of Jesus, be they men or women, he might bring them bound to Jerusalem.

> As Saul came near to Damascus, suddenly a light from heaven shone around him. Saul fell to the earth and heard a voice saying to him, "Saul, Saul, why do you persecute me?"

> Saul said, "Who are you, Lord?"

> The Lord said, "I am Jesus, the one you persecute. It is hard to swim against the current."

Trembling and astonished, Saul said, "Lord, what will you have me do?"

The Lord said, "Get up and go to Damascus. There, you will be told what to do."

56

Jesus said:

Whoever has studied the world has discovered a corpse;
Whoever has discovered a corpse, the world is not worthy of that one.

Meditation

"Studied" may also be translated as "discovered." Rather than being a condemnation of the flesh or of material reality, this saying describes a step toward realization. Just as the Buddhist master Dogen stared at a wall, the Christian mystical tradition called "*via negativa*," the way of negation, has focused on thought beyond that created by objects. As the author of *The Cloud of Unknowing* puts it,

> But now you ask me: "How will I think on God? What is God?" To this I cannot answer you except like this: "I do not know." Consider: your question brings me into that same darkness, and into that same cloud of unknowing, that I hope you will enter.

> Consider: of all other creatures and their works—yes, and even of the works of God—a person may, through grace, fully understand them. We can think about those things. On the other hand, no one can think about God. So I leave behind all the things that I can think about and choose instead to love that thing that I cannot conceive of. For God may be loved, but not thought. So, by love God may be gotten and held, but God cannot be either gotten or held by thought. Therefore, though it is good sometimes to think of the kindness and worthiness of God—and that is an element of contemplation—nevertheless in this work the kindness and worthiness of God will be cast down and covered with a cloud of forgetting.

You will step above these things stalwartly, though wisely, with a devout and pleasing stirring of love, attempting to pierce that darkness above you. You will smite that thick cloud of unknowing with a sharp dart of longing love, and you will not stop, no matter what happens. (Chapter 6)

57

Jesus said:

The Dance of the Sacred is like a person who has sown good seed;
> but an enemy came in the night and sowed weeds over the good
> seed.

The person did not allow anyone to pull up the weeds, saying,
> "You will go to pull up the weeds, but will pull up the good seeds
> as well.
> At the time of harvest, the weeds will be plain to see.
> Then we will pull them up and burn them."

Meditation

Followers of The Way must learn what in Buddhism is called "non-discrimination." In Matthew 7:1–2 Jesus says,

> Judge not, that ye be not judged. For with what judgment
> ye judge, ye shall be judged: and with what measure ye
> mete, it shall be measured to you again. (KJV)

Dogen said,

> In the midst of the Buddhadharma, we are the same Way,
> the same dharma, the same realization, and the same
> practice. Do not speak of others' error and faults. Do not
> destroy the Way. (Loori 79)

58

Jesus said:

Fortunate are those who are troubled; they have found Life.

Meditation

In this text, I have used "fortunate" rather than the more traditional "blessed" for these sayings. Added together, they make up what has traditionally been called The Beatitudes, which appear, in varied form, in the Gospels of Matthew and Luke. Here is Luke 6:20-26:

> Then he looked up at his disciples and said:
> "Blessed are you who are poor, for yours is the kingdom of God.
> Blessed are you who are hungry now, for you will be filled.
> Blessed are you who weep now, for you will laugh.
> Blessed are you when people hate you, and when they exclude you, revile you, and defame you on account of the Son of Man.
> Rejoice in that day and leap for joy, for surely your reward is great in the sky; for that is what their ancestors did to the prophets.
> But woe to you who are rich, for you have received your consolation.
> Woe to you who are full now, for you will be hungry.
> Woe to you who are laughing now, for you will mourn and weep.
> Woe to you when all speak well of you, for that is what their ancestors did to the false prophets. (NRSV)

59

Jesus said:

Keep in mind living while you are living
lest, when you die, you begin seeking
and cannot find.

Meditation

Theologian Paul Tillich said,

> The name of this infinite and inexhaustible depth and
> ground of all being is God. That depth is what the word
> God means. And if the word has not much meaning for
> you, translate it, and speak of the depths of your life, of the
> source of your being, of your ultimate concern, of what you
> take seriously without any reservation. Perhaps, in order to
> do so, you must forget everything traditional that you have
> learned about God, perhaps even that word itself.

60

There was a Samaritan carrying a lamb and going to Judea.

Jesus asked his followers: Why is that man carrying a lamb?

His followers said to Jesus: So that he can kill it and eat it.

Jesus said to them: While the lamb is alive, the man will not eat it; rather, he will eat it after the lamb has become a corpse.

His followers said: That is the only way.

Jesus said to them: You yourselves must seek a place of stillness, lest you be killed and eaten.

Meditation

Genesis 11 relates this story:

> Now all the world had a common tongue,
> speaking one language.
> As they came from the east
> they found a plain in the land of Sinar
> and they settled there.
>
> People said one to another, Come on
> let us make brick and burn it with fire.
> So they used brick as their stone
> and slime as their mortar.
>
> They said, Come on
> let us build a city and a tower
> whose top reaches heaven.

Let us make a name for ourselves
Lest we be scattered about over all the earth.

YHWH came down to see the city
and the tower that the children of Adam were building.
YHWH said, "See
the people are one
and have a common tongue among them.
Now they have begun to do this
and will not leave off
from all that they have purposed to do.
Come on,
let us go down and mangle their tongue
so that one will not know what another says."

Thus YHWH scattered them from thence all over the earth.
So the people left off building the city.
This is why it is called Babel,
because there YHWH confounded the tongue of all the
    world
and because YHWH scattered them from there
over all the earth.

61

Jesus said:

There will be two on one couch; one will die, the other will live.

Salome said:
> Who are you who climbed onto my couch and ate off my table?

Jesus answered:
> I am the one who comes from the One who is whole. I have received from the One.

Salome said:
> I am your follower.

Jesus said:
> Those who are whole, they are light. However, those who are divided are darkness.

Meditation

Mystic poet William Blake said,

> A fool sees not the same tree that a wise man sees.
> He whose face gives no light, shall never become a star.
> Eternity is in love with the productions of time.
> (*The Marriage of Heaven and Hell*)

62

Jesus said:

I speak of my mysteries to those worthy of my mysteries.
Do not let your right hand know what your left is doing.

Meditation

Zen Master Dahui Zonggao (Ta-hui Tsung-kao) said,

> If you cannot abandon your life, just keep to where your doubt remains unbroken for a while: suddenly you'll consent to abandon your life, and then you'll be done. Only then will you believe that when quiet it's the same as when noisy, when noisy it's the same as when quiet, when speaking it's the same as when silent, and when silent it's the same as when speaking. You won't have to ask anyone else, and naturally you won't accept the confusing talk of false teachers. (Ford 23) (translated by JC Cleary)

63

Jesus said:

There was a rich man who thought,
"I will invest my riches in sowing and reaping,
filling my storehouse with grain
so that I need nothing."

That night, he died.
Those with ears, let them hear.

Meditation

The mystic Julian of Norwich said,

> Lord Jesus, I have heard you say: "Sin is necessary but all
> will be well, and all will be well, and every kind of thing
> will be well."

64

Jesus said:

A man had some visitors. When dinner was ready, the man sent his servant to call the visitors.

The servant went to the first and said, "My master calls you."

The first one said, "I have to pay some traders and order some things. I cannot come to dinner."

The servant went to the second and said, "My master calls you."

The second said, "I have just bought a house and must complete the deal. I cannot come to dinner."

The servant went to the third, saying, "My master calls you."

The third one said, "My friend is getting married and there is a party. I cannot come tonight."

The servant went to another, saying, "My master calls you."

That one said, "I have just bought a farm and have to pay the taxes. I cannot come."

The servant came back to the master and said, "Those you invited have all begged off."

The master said, "Go outside to the road and invite to my dinner anyone you meet."

Buyers and traders will not meet the One.

Meditation

The *Upanishads* contain these verses:

Those who depart
From this world
Without knowing
Who they are or
What they truly desire
Have no freedom here
Or hereafter. (Chandogya Upanishad VIII.1.6)

65

Jesus said:

A man owned a vineyard.
He hired tenants to work the vineyard for a part of the crop.
The man sent a servant to collect his portion.
The tenants grabbed the servant and beat him.
Another went, and they nearly killed him.

The man thought, "Perhaps they did not know who he was."
He sent another servant, but the tenants beat that one too.
Then the man sent his son, saying,
"Perhaps they will be ashamed when they see my son."

But the tenants, knowing the son to be the heir to the vineyard,
seized him and killed him. Those with ears, let them hear.

Meditation

Those who value tradition, the letter of the law over the spirit, will kill
those with a new message.

In the twelfth chapter of the *Gospel According to Mark* the enemies of
Jesus say,

> Rabbi, we know that you are sincere and bow before no
> one because you care not for human laws but for the truth
> of God.

In his poem "Ode: Intimations of Immortality" Romantic poet William
Wordsworth said,

> But trailing clouds of glory do we come
>   From God, who is our home:
> Heaven lies about us in our infancy!

Shades of the prison-house begin to close
  Upon the growing Boy,
But He beholds the light, and whence it flows,
  He sees it in his joy;
The Youth, who daily farther from the east
  Must travel, still is Nature's Priest,
  And by the vision splendid
Is on his way attended;
At length the Man perceives it die away,
And fade into the light of common day.

66

Jesus said:

Show me the stone the builders refused; that is the cornerstone.

Meditation

This saying ends the Parable of the Vineyard in Mark. The lines are a quotation from Psalm 118:22.

Liberation Theology, first articulated by Father Gustavo Gutierrez, teaches a "preferential option for the poor." Fr. Gutierrez said, "Real Christian love is founded on commitment to a more just society and action to bring it about."

67

Jesus said:

Those who know all
But not themselves
Know nothing.

Meditation

Philosopher Emmanuel Kant said, "Enlightenment is escape from self-inflicted immaturity."

68

Jesus said:

Fortunate are you when you are hated and persecuted.
Those who persecute you will never find a place.

Meditation

Theologian Paul Tillich argued that faith requires risk and doubt:

> Faith consists in being vitally concerned with that ulti-
> mate reality to which I give the symbolical name of God.
> Whoever reflects earnestly on the meaning of life is on the
> verge of an act of faith.

69

Jesus said:

Fortunate are those who persecute themselves,
for they truly know The One.

Fortunate are the hungry,
for the bellies of the hungry will be filled.

Meditation

The second part of this saying is one of The Beatitudes. As a follow-up to
Saying #68, the first part of this saying turns the pointed finger around
to the self.

70

Jesus said:

When you think for yourself, you save yourself.
That which you do not have in you will kill you.

Meditation

The bedrock belief of the Wisdom Way is that ultimate truth is available to each individual without external interference. The external, Jesus says here, is deadly. You must rely upon yourself.

Philosopher Andre Comte-Sponville said,

> Being is mystery, not because it is hidden or because it hides something but, on the contrary, because self-evidence and mystery are the same thing, because the mystery is *being* itself." (143) (Sponville's italics)

71

Jesus said:

I will destroy this house,
and no one will rebuild it,

ever.

Meditation

According to The *Gospel of Mark*, Jesus was tried for saying that he would destroy the Temple and rebuild it in three days. In that Gospel, this was a false accusation: "We heard him say, 'I will destroy this temple that is made with hands, and within three days I will build another made without hands.'" Mark had reported Jesus to say both that the Temple would be destroyed and that he himself would be killed and would in three days come back from the dead. In an odd twist on the false accusation, later Christians speculated that the Temple had become the body of Christ, the resurrected Jesus. Here, without a biographic context, the saying becomes even more odd. Is Jesus looking at the Temple when he says this? Since *The Gospel of Thomas* seldom offers context, we do not know. Yet, since the saying is offered without context, perhaps it is about something else.

A Zen Buddhist tale tells of Master Ryokan who lived in utter poverty in a tiny hut. One night while Ryokan was away a thief rifled through the hut but could find nothing to steal. Ryokan came back, meanwhile, and warmly greeted the thief who was too surprised to run. Ryokan wanted to give the thief something, but all he had was the robe he was wearing. Ryokan took it off, handing it to the thief, who, surprised, took the robe and ran. Ryokan sat down, naked, and noticed the full moon out his window. "I wish I could have given him that, too," said Ryokan.

72

Someone said to Jesus:

Speak to my brothers so that they will divide our father's estate with me.

Jesus said:
  Who made me a divider?

Jesus turned to his followers and said:
  Seriously—am I a divider?

Meditation

Though the canonical Gospels describe Jesus as someone who loved eating with a great variety of people, *The Gospel of Thomas* shows little of the humanity of Jesus. This saying is a glimpse of the humor of Jesus. Since this text displays Jesus teaching the oneness of the all, Jesus appears to be poking fun at himself here.

73

Jesus said:

The harvest is plentiful;
The laborers are few;

Pray for laborers
For the harvest.

Meditation

St. Francis of Assisi once said,
    "Wherever you go, preach. Use words if necessary."

74

Someone said:

Oh, lord, there are many around the well but no water inside.

Meditation

Religious traditions
Are at once used up—
A dry cistern—and a
Fresh-flowing spring
Waiting to be found—
Always the death rattle
And the "beginning
Of birth pangs" at once

75

Jesus said:

There are many standing at the door,
But only those who are alone
Will enter into the wedding feast.

Meditation

The emphasis on being alone recurs in *The Gospel of Thomas*, indicating that the practice of silence was probably part of the thinking of this religious movement.

Philosopher Rudolph Steiner said,

> To be free is to be capable of thinking one's own thoughts—not the thoughts merely of the body, or of society, but thoughts generated by one's deepest, most original, most essential and spiritual self, one's individuality.

76

Jesus said:

The Dance of the Sacred is like a merchant who had a consignment.
The merchant found a pearl.
He was wise and so sold the consignment and bought the pearl
  for himself.

You, also, should seek after treasure that does not rot,
a place no moth approaches and no worms destroy.

Meditation

Matthew 13:45-46 contains the story of the "pearl of great price." In this version of the parable the merchant is not a dealer in pearls but recognizes a valuable object when he sees it. Franz Kafka said,

> You do not need to leave your room. Remain sitting at your table and listen. Do not even listen, simply wait. Do not even wait, be quite still and solitary. The world will freely offer itself to you to be unmasked, it has no choice, it will roll in ecstasy at your feet.

77

Jesus said:

I am the light over all lights.
I am the all;

the all comes from me
and all goes back to me.

Split wood and find me there;
lift a stone and find me there.

Meditation

Walt Whitman said in *Leaves of Grass*,

> I bequeath myself to the dirt to grow from the grass
>   I love,
> If you want me again look for me under your boot-soles.
>
> You will hardly know who I am or what I mean,
> But I shall be good health to you nevertheless,
> And filter and fibre your blood.
>
> Failing to fetch me at first keep encouraged,
> Missing me one place search another,
> I stop somewhere waiting for you.

78

Jesus said:

Why did you come to the field?
To watch a reed moving in the wind?
To watch the rulers and the powerful
In their fancy clothes?

Those in expensive garments
Will never know the truth.

Meditation

Jesus makes no bones about his preference for the poor and his disdain
for wealth.

Father Thomas Merton, in his book based on the Fourth Century writings of the early monastics, *The Wisdom of the Desert*, reports:

> A brother asked one of the elders: How does fear of the
> Lord get into a man? And the elder said: If a man have
> humility and poverty, and judge not another, that is how
> fear of the Lord gets into him. (27)

79

A woman in the crowd said:

Fortunate is she who bore you, she whose breasts nourished you.

Jesus said to the woman:

Fortunate are they who have listened to the word of the One and done it. The days will come when you will say, "Fortunate is she who did not bear children, she whose breasts never nourished."

Meditation

Poet Charles Bukowski says, "You begin saving the world by saving one person at a time; all else is grandiose romanticism or politics."

80

Jesus said:

Whoever has known the world
Has found the body;

Whoever has found the body, however—
The world is not worthy of that one.

Meditation

Buddhist priest Ajahn Chah was once asked about delusion. "I can understand anger and greed," said the student, "but how do I observe delusion?"

Ajan Chah responded, "You are riding a horse and asking 'Where is the horse?' Pay attention!"

81

Jesus said:

Those who have become rich,
let them become kings,

and those who have power,
let them abdicate.

Meditation

Mark, in the tenth chapter, relates this story:

> Later, when Jesus was walking on the road, a man came running up and kneeled before him, asking him, "Good rabbi, what should I do so that I may inherit eternal life?"
>
> Jesus said to the man, "Why do you call me good? No one is good but God. You know the commandments—Do not commit adultery; do not kill; do not steal; do not bear false witness; defraud not; honor your father and mother."
>
> The man said, "Rabbi, I have observed these laws since my youth."
>
> Filled with compassion, Jesus looked at the man and said, "You lack one thing: go your way, sell whatever you have, give it to the poor, and you shall have treasure in heaven. Then, come follow me."
>
> The man was sad at that saying and went away grieved, for he had a great number of possessions.

Jesus looked around at his disciples and said, "It will be hard for those with riches to enter into the kingdom of Heaven!"

The disciples were astonished at his words. But Jesus answered, saying, "Children, it is so hard for those who trust in wealth to enter into the kingdom of God! It is easier for a camel to go through the eye of a needle than for the rich to enter into the kingdom of God."

82

Jesus said:

Those close to me
Are close to the fire;

Those far from me
Are far from the Dance.

Meditation

Though this saying hints toward the extremely damaging sentiment of
John 14:6 ("No one comes to the Father except through me"), *The Gospel
of Thomas* argues against that narrow definition. Christian tradition has
too often seen the teachings of Jesus—or, more properly understood,
the dogmatic belief in a particular understanding of the message of
Jesus—as the only key to a locked gate. When we remove the question of
belief, seeing religious practice as the practice itself—doing rather than
believing—the gate is gateless.

83

Jesus said:

People see images but not the light in them.
The light of the One is hidden in the image,
though it will be revealed.

The image of The One
is hidden in the light of The One.

Meditation

Christian hermeticist and mystic Valentin Tomberg said,

> Contemplation—which follows on from concentration and
> meditation—commences the very moment that discursive
> and logical thought is suspended. Discursive thought is
> satisfied when it arrives at a well-founded *conclusion*. Now,
> this conclusion is the *point of departure* for contemplation.
> It fathoms the *profundity* of this conclusion at which dis-
> cursive thought arrives. Contemplation discovers a world
> *within* that which discursive thought simply verifies as
> "true." (44. Italics those of Tomberg)

84

Jesus said:

Seeing your own likeness makes you happy.
However, when you look upon your image
that came into being before your birth
and that will not die, how much can you bear?

Meditation

A Zen koan considers that same idea:

What did your face look like before your parents were born?

85

Jesus said:

Adam came into being out of
great power and great wealth,

yet he is not worthy of you.
Else, he would not have tasted death.

Meditation

Jesus is not here reflecting the later concept of Original Sin, though he is
drawing a distinction between what is made and that which is not made,
or conditioned.

The author of *The Cloud of Unknowing*, following the tradition of a writer now known as Pseudo-Dionysus the Areopagite, sees this difference
as fundamental to mystical understanding. The author of *The Cloud of
Unknowing* distinguishes between what can be said, communicated, or
understood with the "blabbering fleshly tongue" capable only of com-
municating through opposites such as "up or down, in or out, behind or
before, on one side or on another other" and that which can be known
only in "the cloud of unknowing," a dark place of complete rejection of
the material world and therefore, one hopes, complete connection to the
divine.

86

Jesus said:

Foxes have their dens
and birds have their nests;

the child of humanity, however,
has no place to lay his head and rest.

Meditation

The social dislocation of Jesus was considerably rarer in his time, and therefore more scandalous. The author of *The Gospel According to Mark* relates this scene:

> When they heard the story that Jesus had an unclean spirit, his brothers and mother came to see him. When they were outside the house, they sent a message to him. The crowd around Jesus said, "Look, your mother and your brothers are outside looking for you."
>
> Jesus answered, "Who is my mother or my brothers?" Jesus looked around at those gathered and said, "Just look at my mother and my brothers! Whoever does the will of God is my brother and my sister and my mother."

87

Jesus said:

Wretched is a body that depends upon the body
and the soul that depends upon these two.

Meditation

Buddhist and psychologist Jack Kornfield writes,

> We must find in ourselves a willingness to go into the dark,
> to feel the holes and deficiencies, the weakness, rage, or
> insecurity that we have willed off in ourselves. We must
> bring a deep attention to the stories we tell about these
> shadows, to see what is the underlying truth. Then, as we
> willingly enter each place of fear, each place of deficiency
> and insecurity in ourselves, we discover that its walls are
> made of untruths, or old images of ourselves, or ancient
> fears, or false ideAs of what is pure and what is not. We will
> see that each is made from a lack of trust in ourselves, our
> hearts, and the world. (194)

88

Jesus said:

The angels and the prophets come to you,
giving you what you have already.
You yourselves give them what you have,
saying to yourselves,
"When will they come and take what is theirs?"

Meditation

Mystic understanding always insists that the self is already sufficiently equipped to comprehend itself and divine reality. As the author of *The Cloud of Unknowing* puts it,

> But yet—all reasonable creatures, angel and human, have in them each one a principal working power, which is named a knowledgeable power, and another principal working power, which is named a loving power. As for these two powers, to the first, which is a knowing power, God, that is the maker of them, is always incomprehensible; but to the second, which is the loving power, in each one diversely God is completely comprehensible, insomuch that one loving soul only in itself, by virtue of love, should comprehend in it God—that is sufficient to the full and much more, without comparison—to fill all the souls and angels that ever may be. (Chapter 4)

89

Jesus said:

Why wash the outside of a cup?
Do you not understand that
whoever created the inside
created the outside also?

Meditation

Chapter 11 of the *Tao Teh Ching* includes these lines,

> We make a pot from a lump of clay;
> Yet it is the empty space
> Within the pot that makes it useful. (15)

90

Jesus said:

Come to me,
for my yoke is light,
my lordship gentle.

You will find rest.

Meditation: Making Everything Fit

> I thought I'd cut off
> Just this much
> Since I thought
> That would help
> Getting everything
> Into the box
> And then I thought
>
> I'd cut off
> Just this much more
> First an arm
> Then a leg
> Then another
> And the other
> So everything would fit
>
> Into the box
> I thought I'd cut off
> Just that much
> I thought
> And that was
> The mistake
>
> I thought

91

They said to Jesus:

Tell us who you are so that we may believe you.

Jesus said:
> You read the face of sky and earth,
> yet you do not see who is right here.
>
> You do not know how to read
> what is happening here, now.

Meditation

Since *The Gospel of Thomas* contains no miracles, no exorcisms, no crucifixion, and no resurrection, the message of Jesus in this text stands only on its usefulness toward the goal of enlightened living. The message: open your eyes.

In Chinese tradition, when Bodhidharma, a Buddhist monk from India, brought his message to China, the Emperor Wu, a student of Buddhism, failed to grasp Bodhidharma's reply to his question, "Who are you that I am seeing?" Bodhidharma said, "I do not know." Emperor Wu later regretted failing to understand the depth of this answer and erected a memorial to Bodhidharma with an inscription that read in part,

> As long as the mind dwells
> On the appearances
> It dwells in the dark.
> When the mind embraces the void
> It climbs the throne of Enlightenment.

92

Jesus said:

Seek and you will find.
In the past I did not answer
when you asked me.

Now, I wish to tell,
but you do not ask.

Meditation

The human propensity toward autopilot can have devastating consequences.

READING THE SIGNS

    Because we did not read the signs—
    Neither in graffiti nor tattoo;
    Neither writ in laughter nor blood;

    Because we learned to see
    —whether blood or laughter—
    Without seeing . . .

    Because we could not
    Read the signs,
    There was evening
    And morning, but
    There was no day.

    And Elohim blessed them;
    And Elohim beheld all;
    And, lo, all was good.
    But we would not see the signs.

117

Comes in,
A gentle summer rain;
No breeze and
Airplanes off
Into morning clouds,

But there is no evening
And there is no morning.

And even so it is.

93

Jesus said:

Do not give what is holy to dogs
since it will end up in manure;

do not throw pearls to swine.

Meditation

Emperor and philosopher Marcus Aurelius said,

> With each thing you do,
> pause to ask yourself:
> Is death a dreadful thing
> because it deprives me of this?

94

Jesus said:

Seek and you will find; knock and you will be let in.

Meditation

Confucius said, "Is Goodness indeed so far away? If we really wanted Goodness, we should find that it was at our side."

95

Jesus said:

If you have money,
do not lend it at interest.
Rather, give it to someone
you know will not give it back.

Meditation

The Dance of the Sacred is a realm in which freely giving is the rule rather than the exception. The Koran says, in 2:274,

> Those that give alms by day and by night, in private and in public, shall be regarded by their Lord. They shall have nothing to fear or to regret. (40)

96

Jesus said:

The Dance of the Sacred is like
a woman who took a little yeast
and hid it in dough. With it,
she made huge loaves of bread.

Those with ears, let them hear.

Meditation

Chinese philosopher Mo-Tzu said,

> The task of the human truly is to seek to promote the benefit of the world and eliminate harm from the world, and to take this as an assumption in the world. Does something benefit people? Then do it. Does it not benefit people? Then stop.

97

Jesus said:

The Dance of the Sacred is like
a woman walking on a road
carrying a jar full of meal.
She did not hear the jar crack,
did not know the meal was
emptying out onto the road.

When she got home,
she put the jar down,
only then seeing
that it was empty.

Meditation

Neither this nor the following parable appears in the canonical Gospels.
Since, unlike the canonical Gospels, *The Gospel of Thomas* offers no in-
terpretation of the parables presented, we have the opportunity to reflect
without preconception, as did the people who heard them from the lips
of Jesus.

98

Jesus said:

The Dance of the Sacred is like
a man who wanted to kill a more powerful man.

The man practiced with his sword at home,
sticking it into the wall.

Then he killed the more powerful man.

Meditation

Poet Keith Waldrop said, "This much seems obvious, that as we move along the path, slowly but certainly the path replaces us."

99

His followers said:

Your brothers and your mother are standing outside.

Jesus said to them:

Those here who do the will of the One
are my brothers and my mother.
They will enter the Dance of the Sacred.

Meditation

See saying #86. Mark adds this bit of biographical detail:

> When they heard the story that Jesus had an unclean spirit, his brothers and mother came to see him.

Psychologist Carl Jung said,

> Unfortunately there can be no doubt that man is, on the whole, less good than he imagines himself or wants to be. Everyone carries a shadow, and the less it is embodied in the individual's conscious life, the blacker and denser it is. If an inferiority is conscious, one always has a chance to correct it. Furthermore, it is constantly in contact with other interests, so that it is continually subjected to modifications. But if it is repressed and isolated from consciousness, it never gets corrected. (*Psychology and Religion*)

100

They showed a gold coin to Jesus and said:

Caesar's agents demand taxes from us.

Jesus said to them:
    Give Caesar what is Caesar's;
    give God what is God's.
    And give me what is mine.

Meditation

The final sentence is not contained in other versions. Is it a joke?

What obligation do those who wish to live in the kingdom of Heaven (the Dance of the Sacred) have toward human political structures? According to the gospel writers, Jesus condemned the Jewish leaders of his day—collaborators with the Roman occupation authorities. Perhaps an idea from Paul provides some light:

    God chose the low,
    The despised—
    What is not—
    To break to nothing
    All that is. (1 Corinthians 1:28)

101

Jesus said:

Those who do not hate father and mother as I do
cannot become my followers; those who
do not love father and mother as I do
cannot become my followers. My mother
gave birth to me; she gave me life but not

The life.

Meditation

The *Upanishads* contain these lines,

> You are what
> Your deep, driving
> Desire is. As
> Your desire is,
> So is your will.
> As your will is,
> So is your deed.
> As your deed is,
> So is your destiny. (Brihadaranyaka IV:4-5)

102

Jesus said:

Cursed are the religious authorities,
for they are like a dog resting in a manger.

The dog neither eats
nor allows the oxen to eat.

Meditation

See saying #39.

Ralph Waldo Emerson said, "What we are, that only can we see.

Aesop also uses the metaphor:

PANTOUM ON THE DOG IN THE MANGER

> A dog once for its nap jumped into a manger,
> Nestling itself into the soft hay.
> When he got home from work, tired and hungry,
> The ox found the dog there,
> Nestling itself into the soft hay.
>
> "If you come close, I will bite," barked the dog.
> The ox found the dog there.
> The ox said, "But you don't even eat hay!"
> "If you come close, I will bite," barked the dog.

When he got home from work, tired and hungry,
The ox said, "But you don't even eat hay!"

A dog once for its nap jumped into a manger.

103

Jesus said:

Fortunate are those who know where the thieves come in so that they may prepare themselves.

Meditation

The author of *The Cloud of Unknowing* said,

> Work on then, I beseech you, quickly. Look forward now and let backwards go. Pay attention to what you lack, not what you have: for that is the easiest getting and keeping of meekness. It behooves you greatly to stand now in desire so that you will profit by the degree of your perfection. It behooves you greatly now because it has been wrought in your will by the hand of Almighty God and you have consented. But one thing I will tell you: God is a jealous lover and allows no other relationships and God will not work in your will except God be only with you, all alone.
>
> God asks help from none but yourself. God asks only that you look on God and let God alone. You are asked to keep the windows and the door from assailing flies and enemies. And if you are willing to do this, you need but meekly to ask God in prayer and soon God will help you. Get started, then: see how you get on. God is very ready and only waits for you.
>
> But what will you do and how will you begin? (Chapter 2)

104

They said to Jesus:

Come, pray and fast today.

Jesus said:
> What have I done wrong?
> How have I lost the battle?
> When the bridegroom is gone,
> then will be the time to

fast and pray.

Meditation

In his book *Cutting Through Spiritual Materialism,* Tibetan Buddhist Chogyam Trungpa famously called the trappings of religious practice "spiritual materialism." The bells and smells of various religious practices contribute more to the egos of practitioners than their spirit.

105

Jesus said:

Whoever knows both father and mother will be called "child of a whore."

Meditation

Jesus is not kind to familial relationships in *The Gospel of Thomas*. As the most important social structure of the ancient world, the family perhaps appeared to be a stultifying structure at that time. For much of the Western world, this is no longer the case. Still, the process of transformation that Jesus preaches clearly involves breaking through social bonds and culturally-conditioned ways of thinking.

The Dance of the Sacred creates new bonds, relationships, and priorities.

106

Jesus said:

When you make the two one,
you will come to be Children of Humanity.

Then, should you say,
"Mountain, move away!"

it will move.

Meditation

See Saying #48.

Mystic Beatrice Bruteau said,

> The heart of the mystic discovery is that we are all one,
> and that One is unconditioned, unlimited, and undefined.
> This, of course, is the foundation of neighbor love. Once
> we get this realization deep into our psyches, we don't have
> all the usual trouble in loving our neighbors. But until we
> begin to see *ourselves* in *our* undefined reality, we won't
> have the freedom, the power, and the energy to love our
> neighbor in the *neighbor's* undefined reality. (64)

107

Jesus said:

The Dance is like a shepherd with his sheep.
The largest sheep wandered off.
So, the shepherd left ninety-nine sheep
and went searching for the one until he found it.
Then, the shepherd said,
"I love you more than the ninety nine."

Meditation

That "you" is you. A story is told about Rabbi Zushya who, when he was dying, told his students that he was very afraid. His students were shocked and said, "But rabbi, you have always told us that God is full of love and kindness!"

"I'm not afraid of God," said Rabbi Zushya. "I know that God will not ask me why I was not Moses or Isaiah. I'm afraid that God will ask me why I wasn't Zushya."

Christian saint and mystic Francis de Sales said, "Be who you are and be that perfectly well."

108

Jesus said:

Whoever drinks from my mouth,
that person will be as I am;
also, I will become that person,

and the hidden will be revealed.

Meditation

In *Leaves of Grass* Walt Whitman said,

> In me the caresser of life wherever moving, backward as well as
>   forward sluing,
> To niches aside and junior bending, not a person or object
>   missing,
> Absorbing all to myself and for this song.
>
> Oxen that rattle the yoke and chain or halt in the leafy shade, what
>   is that you express in your eyes?
> It seems to me more than all the print I have read in my life.
>
> My tread scares the wood-drake and wood-duck on my distant and
>   day-long ramble,
> They rise together, they slowly circle around.
>
> I believe in those wing'd purposes,
> And acknowledge red, yellow, white, playing within me,
> And consider green and violet and the tufted crown intentional,
> And do not call the tortoise unworthy because she is not something
>   else,

And the jay in the woods never studied the gamut, yet trills pretty
well to me,
And the look of the bay mare shames silliness out of me.

109

Jesus said:

The Dance is like a man who had a treasure in his field that he did not know about. When the man died, he left the field to his son. The son did not know of the treasure either. He sold the field. The new owner plowed the field and found the treasure. He became a wealthy man and loaned out money at interest.

Meditation

We only find the treasure when we plow the field ourselves. As Christian mystic and spiritual-practice teacher Cynthia Bourgeault puts it,

> Whatever theological premises you may or may not choose to believe about Jesus, the primary task of a Christian is not to believe theological premises but to put on the mind of Christ. (*The Wisdom Jesus* 21)

Rev. Bourgeault here refers to *kenosis*, self-emptying, as outlined in Philippians 2:1–8, one of the "Pauline Hymns," which says,

> If then there is any encouragement in Christ, any consolation from love, any sharing in the Spirit, any compassion and sympathy, make my joy complete: be of the same mind, having the same love, being in full accord and of one mind. Do nothing from selfish ambition or conceit, but in humility regard others as better than yourselves. Let each of you look not to your own interests, but to the interests of others. Let the same mind be in you that was in Christ Jesus,
> who, though he was in the form of God,
> did not regard equality with God
> as something to be exploited,
> but emptied himself,
> taking the form of a slave,

being born in human likeness.
And being found in human form,
he humbled himself
and became obedient to the point of death—
even death on a cross. (NRSV)

110

Jesus said:

Those who have found the world and become rich, let them abdicate the world.

Meditation

In his own explanation of the parable of the sower Jesus said,

> Yet, don't you understand the parable? How will you understand the other parables? The sower sows the word. Those on the path hear the words; but when they have heard, Satan comes immediately, and takes away the word that was sown in their hearts. It is like this with words on stony hearts; when they have heard the word, they immediately receive it with gladness; yet they have no root in themselves, and so nourish it only for a short while. Later, when affliction or persecution arises because of the word, they are immediately confounded. And this is how it is with the seeds among thorns: they hear the word, but the cares of this world, and the deceitfulness of riches, and the lusts of other things entering in, choke the word, and it becomes unfruitful. But here is how it is with seeds in good ground: they hear the word, and receive it, and bring forth fruit, some thirtyfold, some sixty, and some a hundredfold. (Chapter 4, *The Gospel According to Mark*)

111

Jesus said:

The sky and the earth
will be rolled up in front of you;
those who live out of The One Who Lives,
those will not see death.

Whoever discovers the world
is superior to the world.

Meditation Based on a Poem by Zen Monk Muso Soseki

Years end ways
I dug and dug

Deeper into the earth

Looking for blue heaven
Choking always

On piles of dust rising

Then once
At midnight
I slipped

And fell into the sky

112

Jesus said:

Cursed is flesh that depends on soul;
Cursed is soul that depends on flesh.

Meditation

The Taoist writer Wei Wu Wei put it this way:

> We ourselves are not an illusory part of Reality; rather are
> we Reality itself illusorily conceived.

113

His followers said to Jesus:

Which day is the Dance coming?

Jesus said:
> It is not coming because
> someone is watching.
> No one will say, "Look, there!"
> or "Look, over there!"

> Rather, the Dance
> Of the Sacred is spread
> out upon the earth.

> People are not looking at it.

Meditation

Yes, the Dance of the Sacred, the kingdom of God, is here. It is not for those unwilling to look. Otherwise, there it is; here it is; it is freely available, everywhere.

As the Sufi poet Rumi put it,

> Out beyond ideas of wrongdoing and rightdoing,
> there is a field. I'll meet you there.

> When the soul lies down in that grass,
> the world is too full to talk about.
> Ideas, language, even the phrase *each other*
> doesn't make any sense.

(from *Essential Rumi*, translated by Coleman Barks)

114

Simon Peter said to them:

Mary should leave us, for women are not worthy of The Life.

Jesus said: Look, I will lead her and make her male so that she herself will be a living spirit resembling you males, for any woman who makes herself male will enter the Dance of the Sacred.

The Gospel According to Thomas

Meditation

See saying #22 for further reflection. Simon Peter clings still to dualistic thinking, in this case a prejudice of his place and time against women. "The Life" appears to refer to the life of an inner-circle follower of Jesus. Breaking the concept down to language Peter will understand (the assumption that males are somehow superior to females), Jesus assures him that women have equal opportunity to enter the Dance of the Sacred.

Conclusion

One who speaks does not know;
One who knows does not speak. (*Tao Teh Ching*)

No, there is no end to words; and what do they tell us? Finally that, as TS Eliot once said, " . . . the fire and the rose are one."

There's a limit
To the sea
Only
Close to shore

Notes on the Translation

THE AUTHOR HAS REFERRED to the following translations:

The Five Gospels: What Did Jesus Really Say? The Search for the Authentic Words of Jesus, Robert W. Funk, Roy W. Hoover, and the Jesus Seminar, translators. HarperSanFrancisco, 1997.

The Gospel of Thomas translated by Willis Barnstone in *The Other Bible: Ancient Esoteric Texts,* HarperSanFrancisco, 1984.

The Gospel of Thomas: Annotated and Explained by Steven Davies, Skylight Paths Publishing, 2002.

The Gospel of Thomas: The Hidden Saying of Jesus by Marvin Meyer, HarperOne, 1992.

The Gospel of Thomas is one of the texts discovered at Nag Hammadi, Egypt in 1945. The author has striven to be gender-inclusive whenever possible. References to "Father" in reference to God have been changed to "The One."

Sources and Further Reading

Bourgeault, Cynthia. *The Wisdom Jesus: Transforming Heart and Mind—a New Perspective on Christ and His Message*. Boston: Shambhala, 2008.

Bruteau, Beatrice. *Radical Optimism: Practical Spirituality in an Uncertain World*. Boulder: Sentient Publications, 2004.

Comte-Sponville, Andre. *The Little Book of Atheist Spirituality*. New York: Viking, 2007.

Confucius, *The Analects of Confucius*. Translated by Arthur Waley. New York: Vintage, 1938.

Lao Tzu. *Dao De Jing: A Philosophical Translation*. Trans. Roger T. Ames and David L. Hall. New York: Ballantine Books, 2003.

Lao Tzu. *Tao Teh Ching*. Trans. John C.H. Wu. Boston: Shambhala, 1990.

The Dhammadada: the Path of Truth. Trans. by Ananda Maitreya. Parallax Press: Berkeley, 1995.

Ford, James Ishmael and Melissa Myozen Blacker. *The Book of Mu: Essential Writings on Zen's Most Important Koan*. Boston: Wisdom Publications, 2011.

Kornfield, Jack. *A Path with Heart: A Guide Through the Perils and Promises of Spiritual Life*.New York: Bantam, 1993.

Loori, John Daido. *Invoking Reality: Moral and Ethical Teachings of Zen*. Boston: Shambhala, 2007.

The Koran. Trans. N.J. Dawood. London: Penguin, 2003.

Merton, Thomas. *The Wisdom of the Desert Fathers: Sayings from the Desert Fathers of the Fourth Century*. New York: New Directions, 1960.

Tomberg, Valentin (listed as Anonymous). *Meditations on the Tarot: A Journey into Christian Hermeticism*. New York: Putnam, 2002

Winkler, Gershon. *Kabbalah 365: Daily Fruit from the Tree of Life*. Kansas City: Andrews McMeel Publishing, 2004.

The Upanishads. Translated by Eknath Easwaran. Tomales, CA: Nilgiri Press, 2007.